CLIMATE CHANGE
Reef Bleaching

By Chris Muriata

We respect and honour Aboriginal and Torres Strait Islander Elders past, present and future. We acknowledge the stories, traditions and living cultures of Aboriginal and Torres Strait Islander peoples on this land and commit to building a brighter future together.

Library For All Ltd.

What is Climate Change?

Climate change means that the Earth's weather patterns and temperatures are changing. These changes mostly come from people's actions, like burning oil and coal, which releases gases that warm up the planet.

The sun's rays warm the earth.

Burning fuels and other pollutants cause a greenhouse effect in our atmosphere.

More heat stays on Earth, so temperatures rise and weather patterns change. We get stronger storms, heavier rain and longer droughts.

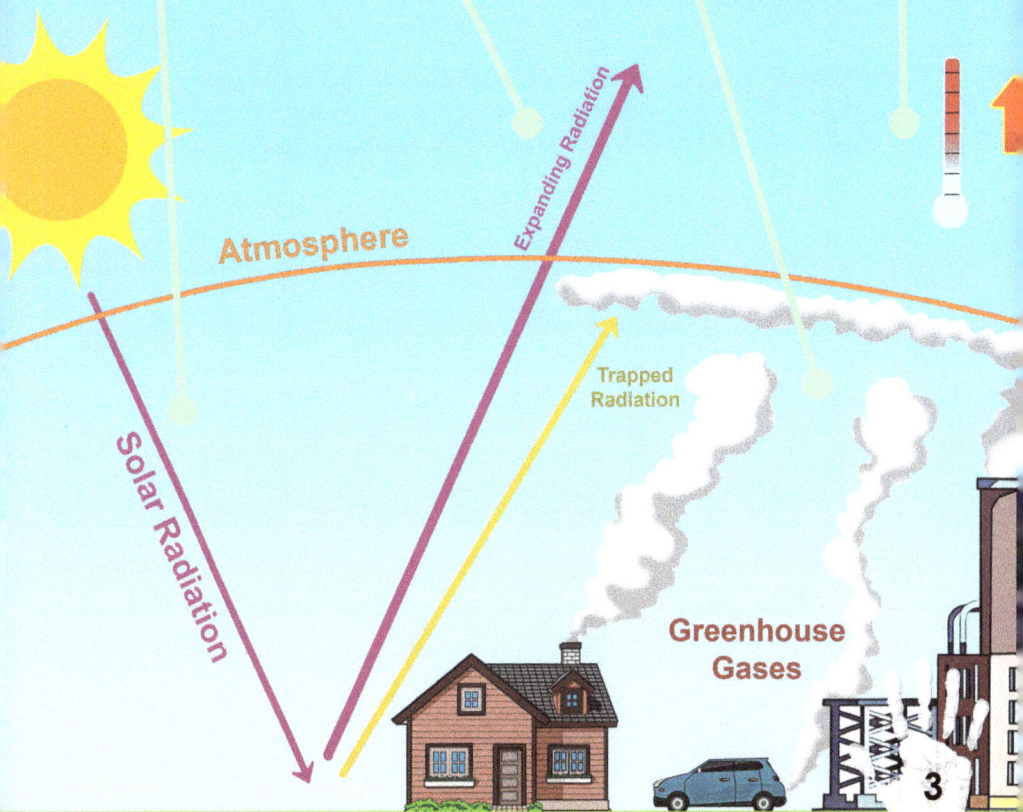

Some heat should stay within our atmosphere, but some escapes into space.

Expanding Radiation

Atmosphere

Trapped Radiation

Solar Radiation

Greenhouse Gases

3

What Is a Reef?

A reef is a ridge of rocks and corals near the surface of the ocean. Reefs provide food and shelter for many ocean organisms, from tiny plankton to large turtles.

Australia's Great Barrier Reef is famous because people like to explore the bright colours of the coral and observe the many sea creatures that live there.

Climate change is making a big difference to the health of our reefs. When a reef gets sick, sea creatures have a hard time finding what they need to survive.

How Does Climate Change Affect the Reef?

When the ocean gets too warm, some of the tiny colourful algae that feed the coral can no longer live there. The coral turns white and becomes vulnerable to disease. This is called reef bleaching.

It only takes a one-degree rise in sea temperature to cause bleaching.

Why Does Reef Bleaching Matter?

A bleached reef struggles to support the fish and plants that live there, making it harder for them to stay healthy and strong. This impacts the whole marine ecosystem.

Around 25% of all marine life live in reefs.

Reef bleaching affects people, too. Damage to plant life and food shortages for sea creatures cause problems for tourism and fishing. Our coasts also become less protected from big waves and storms.

Reef Bleaching

What we've learned so far

1 Reef bleaching happens when the reef is stressed from rising water temperatures.

2 When the water is too warm, the coral pushes out the algae that live inside it.

3 This causes the coral to turn white and lose important nutrients.

4 Small sea creatures who eat algae and plankton have no food or shelter.

5 That means bigger creatures who eat small creatures suffer too.

6 Damage to coral reefs also increases erosion, which increases damage to coastlines.

7 For humans, this impacts fishing programs and tourism.

Community Responses

Not only does a damaged reef affect animals, but it also leaves an impact on people, especially Indigenous communities, who have lived with the reef for thousands of years.

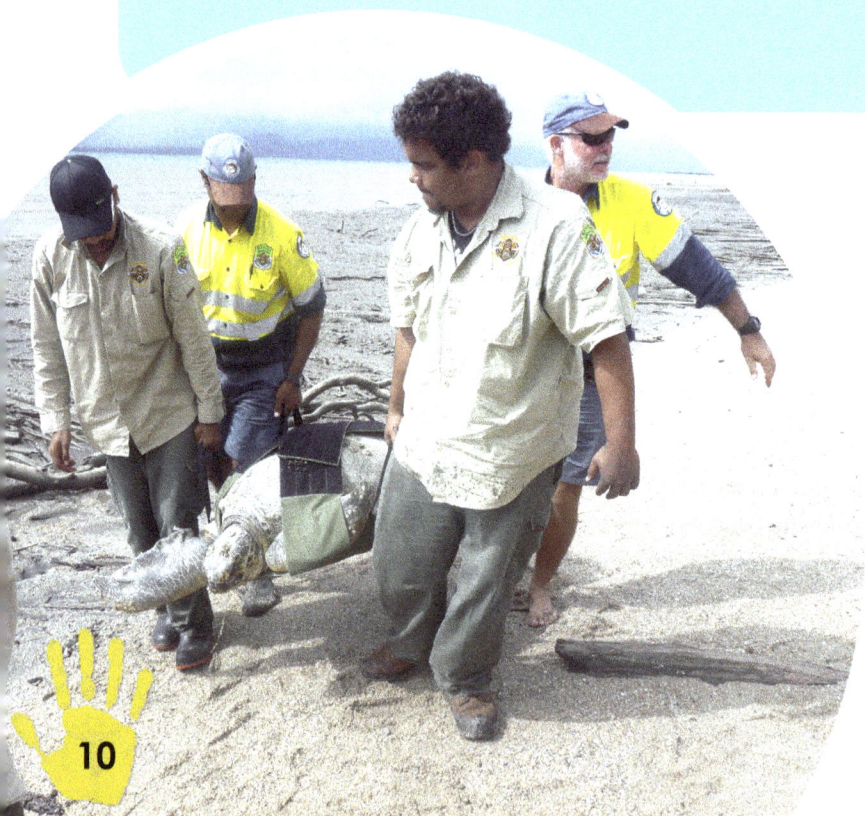

Traditional Ways to Help

Girringun Rangers, who are traditional caretakers, work hard to look after the reef. They use knowledge passed down from their ancestors. They have special rules, like not hunting in certain areas for a while, to help the reef and its creatures heal and stay strong.

The reef is very important to Indigenous communities. It has a deep spiritual and cultural significance; and they rely on it for food and other resources.

Australia's biggest reefs are in Western Australia and North Queensland.

The Great Barrier Reef, visible from space, is the largest living structure on Earth.

Coral reefs are among the most biologically diverse ecosystems on Earth.

Corals have a special partnership with algae, which gives them energy through photosynthesis.

Some reefs can heal from bleaching if conditions get better quickly.

Rangers make records and work with local people and traditional custodians to help the reef as soon as they see problems like bleaching. They restrict activities to give the reef a chance to heal.

Traditional custodians might ban hunting in affected areas to give the ecosystem time to regenerate.

Rangers might limit tourism in affected areas, so there is no further human damage to delicate coral, rocks or plants.

Collaborating on Reef Conservation

Everyone can help fight climate change and protect the reef by doing things like using less energy and supporting rules that help the reef. The wise ways of the First Nations people teach us how to take care of the environment. Their knowledge helps us find better ways to look after the reef and face big challenges together.

Traditional knowledge complements modern scientific approaches by providing insights that guide ecological management and conservation efforts. Traditional owners and Elders work alongside agencies to impose moratoriums and to manage zoning, effectively combining wisdom with contemporary strategies to enhance reef resilience and health.

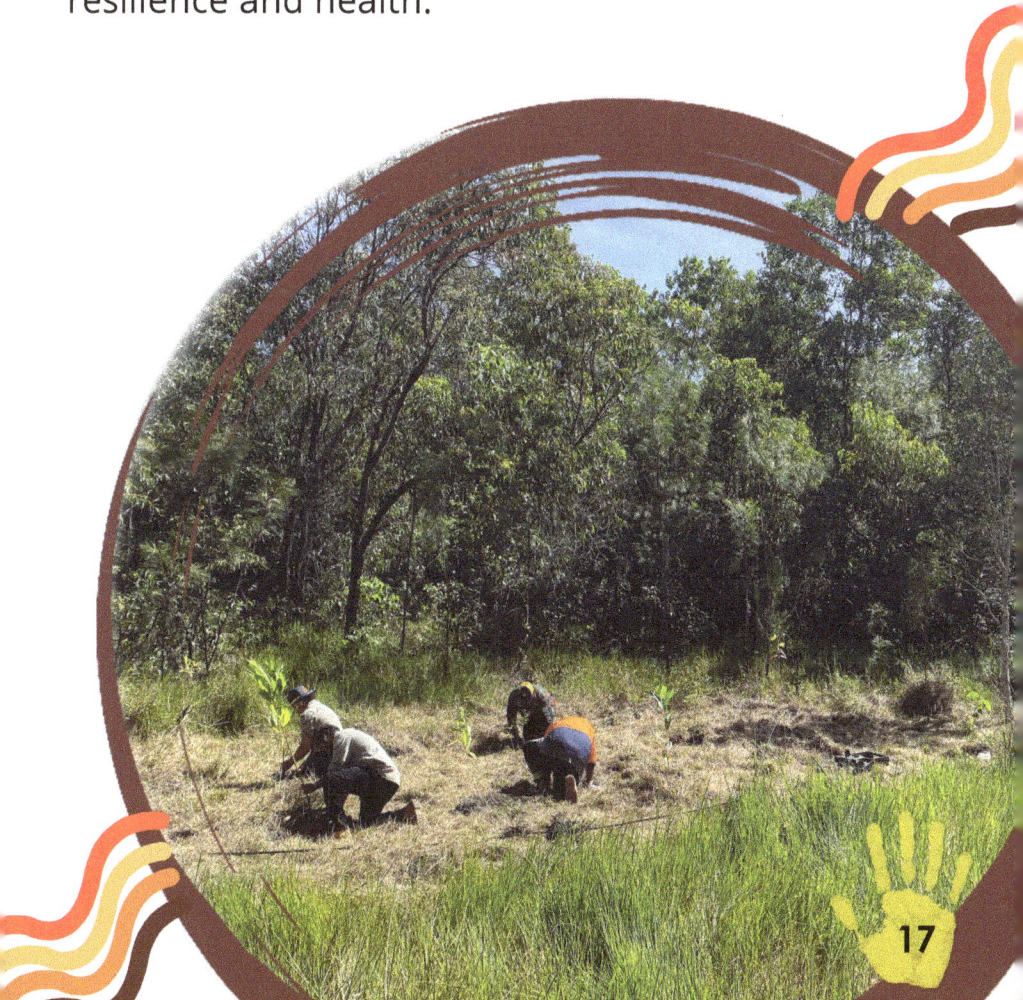

The Biggest Coral Colony

One of the biggest coral colonies ever recorded is a massive Porites coral in the Great Barrier Reef, measuring about 10 metres high and 20 metres wide. Imagine how many sea creatures would be impacted if all of that coral was bleached?

Do the
Reef Quiz

Q What causes global warming?

A Pollution, like carbon dioxide, keeps heat close to Earth, like a greenhouse.

Q How does climate change affect reefs?

A It makes the ocean too warm.

Q What causes coral bleaching?

A When the ocean gets warm, coral expels helpful algae.

Q Why is coral bleaching a problem?

A Bleached coral is fragile and disease prone.

Q How does an unhealthy reef impact marine life?

A Sea creatures lose their home and food source.

Q How does an unhealthy reef impact humans?

A It reduces fishing and tourism, and increases coastal erosion.

Q How do Rangers help the reef?

A They watch carefully, make records, and limit hunting and tourism.

Q How can you help the reef?

A Try to save energy and talk to people around you about ways to help stop pollution.

19

Photo Credits

You can use these questions to talk about this book with your family, friends and teachers.

What did you learn from this book?

Describe this book in one word. Funny? Scary? Colourful? Interesting?

How did this book make you feel when you finished reading it?

What was your favourite part of this book?

Queensland Indigenous Land and Sea Ranger Program

The Queensland Indigenous Land and Sea Ranger Program collaborates with First Nations communities to protect and care for land and sea Country. With over 200 rangers, the program shares cultural knowledge, engages in community education, and leads youth programs like the Junior Ranger initiative, fostering a strong connection to Country and Culture.

Chris Muriata is a Girringun Ranger of the Cardwell community.

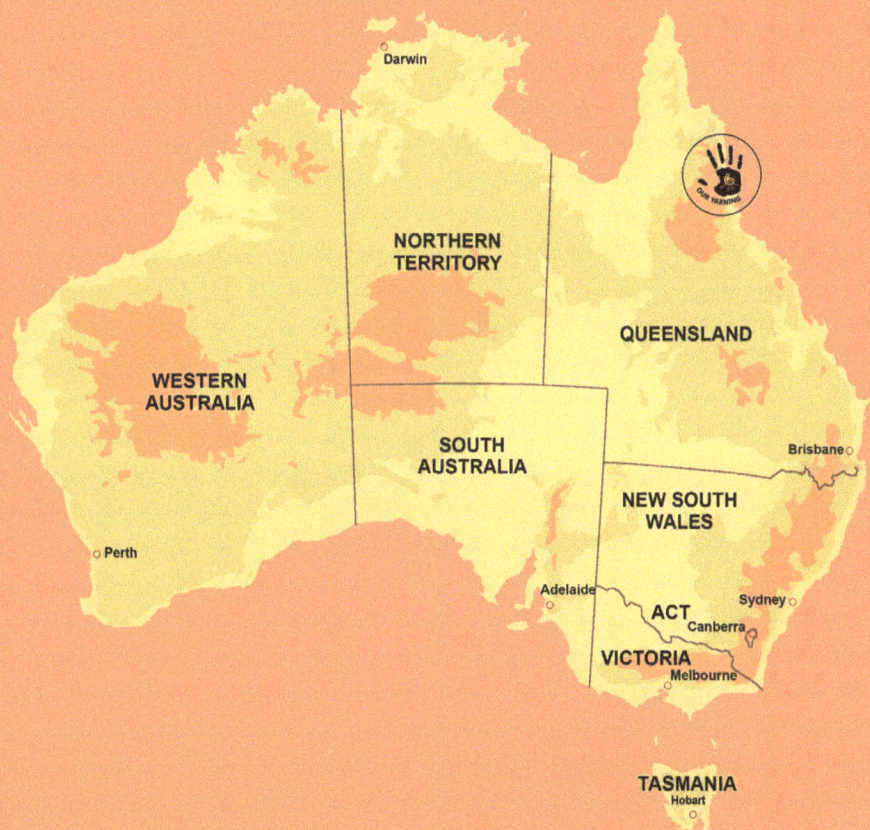

Our Yarning

The Our Yarning collection aligns with the Australian Curriculum through the Cross-Curriculum Priorities — Aboriginal and Torres Strait Islander Histories and Cultures. The collection provides an authentic opportunity for learning and embedding Aboriginal and Torres Strait Islander perspectives because it is written by Aboriginal and Torres Strait Islander people.

We know that children learn better, and enjoy reading more, when they see themselves in the stories, characters and illustrations of the books they read.

To download the app, visit the Google Play Store or Apple Store and search 'Our Yarning'.

libraryforall.org

You're reading Upper Primary

Learner – Beginner readers
Start your reading journey with short words, big ideas and plenty of pictures.

Level 1 – Rising readers
Raise your reading level with more words, simple sentences and exciting images.

Level 2 – Eager readers
Enjoy your reading time with familiar words, but complex sentences.

Level 3 – Progressing readers
Develop your reading skills with creative stories and some challenging vocabulary.

Level 4 – Fluent readers
Step up your reading skills with playful narratives, new words and fun facts.

Middle Primary – Curious readers
Discover your world through science and stories.

Upper Primary – Adventurous readers
Explore your world through science and stories.

Library For All is an Australian not for profit organisation with a mission to make knowledge accessible to all via an innovative digital library solution.
Visit us at libraryforall.org

Climate Change: Reef Bleaching

First published 2024

Published by Library For All Ltd
Email: info@libraryforall.org
URL: libraryforall.org

This project was delivered with the support of QBE under the Community Ready partnership.

This book was made possible with the support of the Queensland Indigenous Land and Sea Ranger Program to support educational outcomes for children in Australia by learning from Indigenous knowledge and stewardship of Country. To learn more, visit https://www.qld.gov.au/environment/plants-animals/conservation/community/land-sea-rangers/locations.

Our Yarning logo design by Jason Lee, Bidjipidji Art

Climate Change: Reef Bleaching
Muriata, Chris
ISBN: 978-1-923207-38-7
SKU04432

www.ingramcontent.com/pod-product-compliance
Lightning Source LLC
Chambersburg PA
CBHW042343040426
42448CB00019B/3390